POETRY BY JAMES HUMPHREY

Paying The Price (1998) VOLUME	*Ice* (1989) CHAPBOOK	
Mize & Kathy (1998) VOLUME	*The Athlete* (1988) VOLUME	
Lef (1997) VOLUME	*After I'm Dead,* *Will My Life Begin?* (1986) VOLUME	*An Homage: The End* *of Some More Land* (1972) CHAPBOOK
SIZ (1997) VOLUME	*In Tribute To Survivors* (1984) CHAPBOOK	*The Visitor* (1972) CHAPBOOK
Bud (1996) VOLUME	*In New York City Air* (1984) CHAPBOOK	*Argument For Love* (1970) VOLUME

Paying the Price

James Humphrey

Poets Alive! Press   1998   New York

Manufactured in the United States of
America
Poets Alive! Press on acid-free paper.

Muriel Rukeyser statement reprinted from
The Speed of Darkness with permission of
the Muriel Rukeyser estate.

Daniel Berrigan, S.J.'s poem *Consolation*,
is reprinted from *And the Risen Bread,
Selected poems, 1957-1997*, Fordham
University Press, 1998. Grateful
appreciation is acknowledged.

Margaret Atwood statements from
her poem *Notes Towards A Poem That Can
Never Be Written*, from her volume of the
same title, published by Oxford University
Press (Canada), 1983. Reprinted by
permission.

The poems *Perfect Acoustics* and *Decision*
are reprinted from *Mize & Kathy*, Poets
Alive! Press, 1998, with permission of
James Humphrey.

Cover/book design and photography:
Saroyan Humphrey

Special limited edition of 500 books.
26 signed/designed "First day of
publication"
by James and Saroyan Humphrey

Humphrey, James, 1939-
     Paying The Price / James Humphrey
     I. Title
ISBN 0-936641-23-1
Acid-free paper

Poets Alive! Press
81 Spruce Street
Yonkers, NY
10701

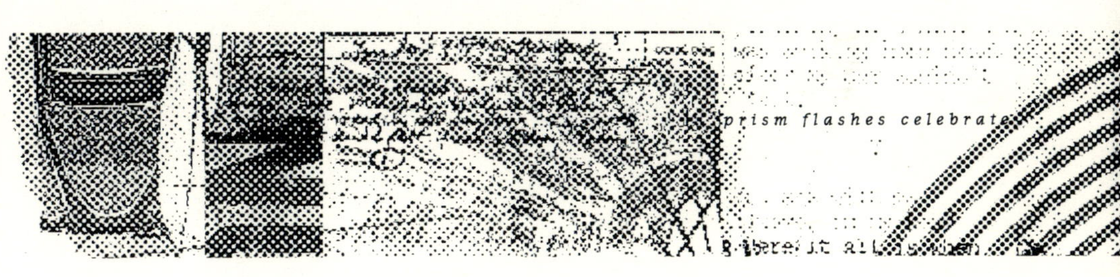
prism flashes celebrate

to be one with my roots

CONTENTS

FOREWORD

U p o n   c o m p l e t i n g   his limited edition five volume
contemporary interpretation sequence of farmland's seasons
and people: *Mize & Kathy*, *Lef*, *Siz*, *Bud*, and *Ice*, each
published by Poets Alive! Press, James Humphrey and his
old Ford headed for the Midwest in search of fresh subject
matter. But as the gods would have it, he drove into a
blizzard almost as soon as he was in Pennsylvania on I-80
West. He really didn't want to write about the weather and
winter anymore, but the storm's perseverance, temporary
beauty—some of it truly rare, and hardships, got him to
writing this collection's first section, *January Night Music*.
Each poem was either written in its entirety when he
experienced it, or the first draft was put on paper then.
Poems that take place outside during the night, the poet
wrote in a thick red sleeping bag wrapped over his parka,
by flashlight or near campfires.

He needed more—maybe something contrasting—to
complete the book. He drove throughout the Midwest
searching for more objective experiences. He talked with
children, teachers, gas station attendants, mechanics,
truckers, waitresses, motel clerks, state troopers, off-duty
detectives, jail inmates, three newspaper journalists, two

poets, and an auctioneer.

During his return trip to New York, Humphrey tried college and university literature departments. No luck. Always a poetry that seemed too abstract and divorced from reality. Discouraged and angry as he left Notre Dame, Indiana, he drove past Holy Cross College and a little voice inside said, "turn around. Give it that proverbial one last try." He did.

There he met the artist Brother Harold Ruplinger, C.S.C. During a seven hour exchange of life experiences, Shakespeare, American coloratura soprano Maria Callas (1923-1977), American painter Robert Henri (1865-1929), famous for his book *The Art Spirit*, and for his realistic works that decried the artificiality and sentimentality of American painting at the turn of the century, different ways college students have changed since the mid-sixties, the Beatles, the homeless, and the danger of art and literature being held on the fringe of our society. Brother Harold said, "What are the different prices people pay to justify their way of living?" Instantly, both knew the muse had spoken with that question. They talked about the prices, including the prices of love, friendship and loyalty. The seed was planted for the second section of this collection: *Paying The Price*.

In our period they say there is free speech.

They say there is no penalty for poets.
There is no penalty for writing poems.
They say this. This is the penalty.

MURIEL RUKEYSER
1913-1980

FROM *The Speed of Darkness*

Paying THE Price

Consolation

Listen
if now and then
you hear the dead
muttering like ashes
creaking like empty
rockers on porches

filling you in   filling you in

like winds in empty
branches   like stars
in wintry trees
so far
so good

you've mastered finally
one foreign tongue

Daniel Berrigan, S.J.

I

january Night Music

January Night Music At Diamond J's

for all the truckers

Ten inches fresh snow.
Now imitating thin stars, feathered castles,
falling through parking lot lights
mountainside off I-80, Pennsylvania.
Engine idles smooth. Heater purrs.

Miles driven last 15 hours
blurred into entering rig's headlights
strafing flat white field. Sparkle of
exaggerated wild oat's stem.

Blood needs to move,
bring me out of daze.

Force mind off road,
dream there is a yellow lady's slipper
in silent field beyond
artificial lights length;
a longhaired beauty there

who will let me pin it on her.

Oh, the perfume of wild flowers,
slender stalks
clumped in her tight fist.

Small reward for the battle of being.

1-98

Daybreak

Grating north wind

Humped shoulders

Heavy trudge

Pickax

Livestock's frozen drinking trough

Outbuilding's loose boards smack

Snow swirls across roofs

Chicken hawk grinds against turbulence

Four wrinkled plums hold on

1-98

PERFECT ACOUSTICS

for Mize

Standing center thick bluish lake

Not breathing

All senses lifted

Stillness never experienced

Bursting from motionless woods

Passionately singing white-throated warbler

No pitch pipe, triangle, metronome,
treble-clef ligature

Nature's perfection unto itself

1-98

Amish Girls Walking To Sunday School

Such literal faces!

Dull wool pilgrim bonnets crowd
ears, hide hair.
Thick black mittens, long bulky
black wool coats.
Black boot soles bite snow,
breaking peace all around.

Oh, where are your youthful tongues,
embarrassed giggles, laughter?
Innocent merriment and mischief,
have you been deserted so early?

*Anyone—do winter stars
hold secret magical dreams?*

Covered bridge.

Church ahead looms larger.

Roaring stone fireplaces.
Girls glowing cheeks.

Safe.

1-98

Symmetry After Snowfall Without Wind

for Linda McCartney
1942-1998

Prism flashes celebrate
each original thin grainy sugar design
filling *every other* square of
woven wire fence

Priceless as the songs inside us
if we reach in for them

grasp them

grow with them

1-98

TEMPLE

Topping packed hill

Child's eyes

Panoramic
always changing
ignited kaleidoscope

Endless
swirling
whirling
forever
twisting
curving
flaring
high-banked
natural mind-blowing
wide-open
perfect 40 sleds wide
Flexible Flyer
racing temple!

The world *all* here!

Silence

All falseness leaves

1-98

REFLECTION

for Saroyan

> The moon
>
> The ice
>
> The ice
>
> The moon
>
> Each
> pressed
> to
> its
> own
> reflection

1-98

4A Ballpark

Glittering ice palace

Single figure skater
Perfect infield ballet

Dreams of spring training

1-98

FRONT PORCH SWING

for Norma

Hard

steady

indifferent wind

Sleet becomes ice
holds supporting chain links forward
Locks them magnified

Wooden seat: stop action glide
smooth
elegant flat pearl

1-98

Sarah Remembers A Special Summer Joy

Changing out of farm woman sweat
into sleeveless polkadot dress,
forearms wild berry thorn scratches,
walks by thick combs
laden with honey and bees.

Short distance ahead, overloaded wagon,
stubborn mules, swarthy driver,
goad-like whip.

Cherokee Indian blurs white pine
on fleet pony sensibly balanced with
dried meats, furs, buffalo robes.

Small, sleek vivid yellow birds,
lime tinted, burst through!
Charms of a sort?

Gentle slope,
chicory waving bright blue blossoms;
asters, hollyhocks, going in
all directions.
Natural celebration of life.

Looking out from slope's summit,
sudden vigorous *OHHHHHHH* sings from her!

Shortleaf pine! Sugar pine! Balsam fir!

How dear
the memory of bringing home
the Christmas tree when a child!

1-98

Somewhere

Somewhere
the Yukon
Northwest Territories
Cumberland Sound

But here

here

farmer's grit, endurance,

gambles as severe

1 - 98

FOUND: ANTIQUE RECIPE BOX

Tilt smooth wooden-hinged lid,
sweet permanent musty smell
floats up.
Flawless ink penmanship on simple paper,
recipe for *Nutmeg, Clove Pumpkin Pie*;
signed Sally Cruthers, 1908,
Maple Sugar Syrup, 1910.
Cybil Brown's *Old Fashioned Tea Cakes*,
1918.
Two different penciled recipes for
Cranberry Frappes, 1921, '25.
Through the Great Depression,
World War II,
nearly 150 original specialties.

More love in here than spoken between
a man and woman today?

1-98

WEIGHT

Concentrated ice
cracks
buckles
thin white trellis

Toppled sunflowers seedless
Stalks coarse

Clothesline empty
sags

Something peers above
ditch needle weeds

Sunset allows
broken
crack
of
candy pink
no one sees

1-98

EARLY NIGHT NEWS

for James Schevill

Stem broken
Colorless glassy clustered crinkleroot
can't
fall

Unrecognizable bird's slight call
lost in winged curve
behind
Northern pitch pine windbreak

Moon—bone white eye

Field hay loaf
majestic muff

1-98

Cabin Fever Breakout

Indestructible laughing

Early teens REVS & REVS
old tractor engine

Dangerous close-together
slanted front tires

Mirror-smooth
corn-stubbled flat field

Blind 25-foot drop to
Wapsipinicon River

Scattered steep, thick
polished rock piles

Forgotten disc harrow
frozen against ground

The challenge

The thrill
The feast

1 - 9 8

In The Distance

Low slanted glass hill
Coarse snow banks
vanish lower trunks
Swedish Birch, Norway Spruce
Sun's rising
a dull orange too long in
kitchen table fruit basket

1-98

Discovery

Basement
younger sisters, brothers
mess with broken Edison Victrola,
fumble ping-pong, loudly
animate board games.

Kitchen
ordinary, mother bastes snow goose.
Daughter's fully-opened mouth
round
pressed tight against ice-streaked window
furthest from stove, warm breath pushing out
forms fog she designs with fingertips,
quickly evaporates.
Makes more and more, breathing harder,
harder—heart's undiscovered blood soaring,
unaware she's after something never felt.

Wished?
Fell
on

purpose?
Full
long
soft
wide
goose
feather
ticklishly
goes
down
blouse
teasing
small
hard
breasts,

shivers.

Beyond blurry window,
no strong, graceful handsome knight
mounted on golden-saddled spirited
white steed,
storybook tellers proclaim to
young girls.
Only the dumb rasping wind
whirling over jagged snow crusts in

dead garden!
Yet instinctively holds onto
center of *her* special mysterious galaxy,
letting dormant pleasures—sensuous perfume,
rush up
out
every pore,
only an eye-blink ahead of mother's order
to help wring another
female snow goose's neck.

1-98

DECISION

for Kathy

Slough
Abstract
frozen common weeds
Dead trees grotesque goblins

Sudden noise

Startled ring-necked pheasant mates
frantic cries
panic into flight

Brief dusk
Pale
Cold
Frightening

Night without light
Through it

Through it

1-98

UNTITLED

Ice-trapped
impassioned purple lovegrass,
lacegrass, angel hair.
Feminine azalea shrub crooked
bone of century woman.

Little distance on,
Kestrel cruises surplus
stacked cordwood.

Sprawling
motionless brambles,
spiny bract porcupine grass
clog cross-railed zigzag fences.

Beyond
Dairy Queen swirl-topped
rolled hay loaves.

Stand of Norway Maple.
Something fluorescent roosting?

red-shafted flicker?

Deeper into unexpected adventures,
herd of fallow deer,
deserted icehouse.
All of it becoming a special pilgrimage
to be one with my roots.

1-98

Prairie Night

Rusted uncut roll barbed wire.
Each barb's size multiplied through
clear ice,
reflects barn's bright pole light.

Doubled-up poverty weed, switchgrass,
bunchberry, moonseed.

High above barn,
nighthawk searches.

Woodchuck hides out.

1-98

MORTALITY

Small
four-legged furred creatures

No more seeds
Stubborn berries
too deep in ice

Instincts w/out dreams

w/out hope

No more strength

Ribs easy to count

Raw stars stay fierce
behind ink black clouds

1-98

By Instinct They Knew One Another

Inside igloo
children's
muffled innocent bursts
giggles
shrill excitement

Who says hummingbirds
don't live in crystal faces

1-98

Field

Weather-split X'd fence posts
barely above vivid white waves

Wild flowers
deep
below
sleep
wait
their
turn

Broken handleless teeter-totter

Leaning windmill
4 blades gone

Sleigh bells

Fir tree bough bends
Plume of snow

1 - 9 8

LESSON 10

for Blue Velvet,
my enduring 1980 Ford Granada,
and for Muriel Rukeyser

If you are an apprentice poet
or a new professional
without a Santa Claus,
accept that it's hard on
your car, money clip, you,
and possibly ending your career,
driving to Midwest,
around in it,
writing winter poems in winter.
It will pit you against
unforeseen, unrelenting tests.
An illustration, LESSON 10.

EVENTUAL SALT DAMAGE TO BLUE VELVET,
JANUARY, 1989, '92, '93, '97, '98:

Replace two rusted-out front doors,

reinforce w/ steel, sand, primer, undercoat:
$525.
Replace entire rocker panel both sides
with steel : $350.
Repair holes in rear wheel wells: $85.

Undercoat entire chassis, floorboards;
each time varied from $325. to $410.
Sand, primer, paint body: $1200.
Rubberized paint for rocker panels: $275.
Assorted parts replacements,
plus tune-ups, oil changes, lubes: $6200.
Total fuel cost? I have no idea.
I use only Amoco premium, adding one quart
Marvel Mystery oil to each 20 gallons,
plus a quart into crankcase with
oil/ filter change every 1500 miles.

January, '98, driving 25 miles to
nearest mechanic after rusted radiator bottom
gave out, destroying water pump
(engine warning light never came on),
before wrapping up in red, down-filled
sleeping bag inside Blue Velvet
waiting for radiator to be shipped in,
for fun of it,

bought single fortune cookie—25¢—
cracked it, withdrew thin slip, read,
"Your heart is given what it needs."

In our period they say there is free speech.

They say there is no penalty for poets.
There is no penalty for writing poems.
They say this. This is the penalty.

MURIEL RUKEYSER
1913-1980

1-98

VETERAN FARMER APPROACHES HIS HOUSE THROUGH DECOMPOSED GARDEN

for Charles Van Vooren
1902-1956

Dill—top-heavy clustered umbels.
Tall stems stiffly move.
Exploded squash, honeydew.
Tramped on zinnias, marigolds.

Closer to house
cedar waxwing lights in old sycamore.
Strikes the man for the first time:
Impossible for tree branches
to outreach their shade...

Jack Frost windows.
Window boxes
—unrecognizable herbs.
Icicles haven't begun.

Weathercock's burned-out face.

Slight fog approaches.

1-98

IMAGINATION MAY BE THE BEST LIFE SAVER WE HAVE

What color has the
outdoor air become?

Why is it so still?

Is the earth gone?

Losing gravity's pull,
trapped in narrowing territory?

Reward *if* survive winter,
its challenges, its suffering
—*richer* crops?

How about letting something rich
permanently bloom in you?

Begin with something simple.

The first time you mow the yard,

will the grass look differently,
or will it be the same old chore?
Will the brave crocus be a nuisance?
What will the showy daffodil be?
The moist rose?

When this storm breaks
Will family meals be prepared
repeating meaningless words about it
to whoever is slicing bread
while someone sets the table,
who in the order of their age,
will recite from memory
their superficial version of it,
reassuring themselves
everything is the same again
—the usual (empty) routine has been saved.
It's all very domestic.

1-98

The Elegance Of All Things

for Georgia O'Keeffe
1887-1986

Through animal pelvis holes
blue sky effortlessly gentle

Surroundings
full-circle cinematography

Splayed red oak
dances silver

Defiant bluebird
puffs chest

Muted bluish-green teal mates
wing through

Apple vines dense
appear to choke,
tenaciously proclaiming exposed

fiery red-coated seeds
Dried arrowroot, arrowhead,
bleeding heart, shepherdess

Persevering twisted jasmine bush,
spiny bract, bristled teasel,
split-open milkweed

Not a sound from the city

No tangle of lives here

Skin breathes clean

1-98

In the dark times
will there also be singing?
Yes, there will be singing
about the dark times.

BERTOLT BRECHT

II

paying the price

9-YEAR-OLD TO AUDIENCE

"I was to dance a happy dance.
Before I came out here,
my father beat me and yelled
I was no good,
and will never amount to anything.

"I hurt too much to dance,
so I'll be a sperm
that falls over dead
—so other children won't
have to be born."

JEAN

Through childhood, adolescence,
did usual daily farm chores
in same way other rural kids did,
not because she wanted to please
her parents, friends, be liked,
or approved, even by herself,
she was following the example set
by her suppressed mother and father.

Natural healthy sex curiosity,
desires,
dreams,
imagination,
asleep.
Parents silence
stings this poet's heart!

Her truths, special abilities,
to be discovered, developed,
keeping her above the rest?

How?

Secrets of her heart to stay mute,
going through a lifetime in the
same community, growing up
with people whose reasons
are never any damn good?
So used to mechanical standard procedures,
not knowing they aren't?
Without a struggle, silently accepting
the masks she ignorantly lives behind
are the real her?

What is the value of a life when its goal
is to be like everybody else?

WORTHY CELEBRATION!

New Year's Eve, '97
in front of vulgarly showy
gambling dens along
Atlantic City's Boardwalk,
hundreds of wealthy women,
many famous,
protesting cruelty to animals,
gave their lavish full-length
fur coats to the homeless.

The giveaway was to continue indefinitely,
spreading to major cities.

Sleep better and longer tonight,
wild mink, seal and otter.
Help is winning!

WILL ONE OF US LOOK BACK AND SEE
THE OTHER LOOKING BACKWARD AT
WHOEVER IS LOOKING BACK, IF EITHER
OF US IS?

Why did we resist
the unique pearls in our throats
the moon's music could have given us?
What happened during our dates
in bright early summer sun,
gentle rainbow meadow strolls
against exciting canvases of early romance?
Were there details to remember;
moments to never forget?

Why didn't we pull open our
rib cages
grasping something called *special,*
or
dig
for
it?

Maybe we both did
when the other wasn't looking,
and found nothing there...

Are we thin, colorless air,
only observers to this lifetime?
Maybe
cowards
is
what
we
really
are.

FOR CAROL COTTON
1939–1974

ONE

Deeply tanned, body spread with
fresh cocoa butter, its sensual smell
arousing in him feelings
never experienced.
Moving like lazy driftwood logs,
the 11-year-old girl and boy
tease crayfish near rounded
small stoned and sand shore of
Minnesota's Big Wadtab lake.

In tender voice, the girl risks saying,
I saw him beating you last night
—that was me who threw the rock
through the window that made him stop.

Shamed, the boy belly-flopped away.
She gave chase.
Catching up, embraced him,

softly repeating, *Its okay...*
It's okay...

Her arms were strong, determined,
withstanding his struggles to escape.
Suddenly, pressed his face into
her neck, sobbing and sobbing,
clinging to her for five hours.

It was the first time in his life
he was given affection.

T W O

September, 1998, he was told
she had died of cancer, cremated,
ashes sprinkled onto the lake shore
where for so many pre-teen tears,
they swam and teased crayfish.

He rushed to her and those permanent
five hours, arms open wide.

40 Years a Poet
September, 1958-1998

The facts of this world seen clearly
are seen through tears

MARGARET ATWOOD

O N E

I wasn't meant to be a poet

Human destiny clearly visioned
in split-second when eight: would play
center field, bat cleanup for the
St. Louis Cardinals,
and become the greatest player of
my time;
then yelled out from bottom of
innermost being,
"WITH THE MONEY I'M GOING TO BUILD
A RANCH FOR BOYS AND GIRLS

WHO GET BEAT UP LIKE ME!"

Age eleven, played junior legion ball
with guys 18 and 22.
Started in center.
Batted cleanup.

A few remember I played one season for
the Cards when 16.
Before 18, could barely touch shoulders
with fingertips.
From 4 until night before left to
catch Greyhound for spring training camp,
JEALOUS, DRUNK, RAGING, STEPFATHER
CREPT UP BEHIND ME,
SAVAGELY BEATING ME WITH A STEEL PIPE,
FOCUSING ON SPINE.
GONE FROM YOUR WRINKLED SKIN,
PERVERSE POWER USELESS IN HELL!

At 20, slowly began rebuilding body toward goal:
give *true* destiny all I had before
complete spinal deterioration and age
stole it.

52,
Permanently, completely blind left eye,
dressed in janitor's uniform,
sporting cloth name patch above shirt pocket,
new roller bucket, fresh mops—works;
with the confidence of a man solid in
blue chip stocks,
begin washing a major league locker room,
gradually mopping toward the tunnel.

On the field, only ten or so players
limbering up in mid-morning sun.
From the mound, a rookie pitcher hurled
into empty batting cage.
I grabbed a bat and jogged to the plate's
left side,
hollered, "I'll be your target!"

Of the next ten pitches, I slammed nine
into the center field bleachers!
As the tenth ball rifled in,
the public address speakers bellowed,
startling me, "GET THAT JANITOR OFF THE
FIELD!

HE DOESN'T EVEN HAVE CLEATS ON—WHO
THE HELL
DOES HE THINK HE IS BUSTIN' IN HERE!"

The hurler yelled toward the glass enclosed
offices half-way to heaven, "DID YOU SEE
WHAT HE JUST DID?"
The PA system boomed back:
"HE'S ONLY A BROOM PUSHER!
NOW GITTIM' OUTTA' HERE!
HE'S FIRED!"

T H R E E

Cheated at birth,
writing all that was left me.
Painting, sculpting too expensive.
Living in cardboard boxes,
pencil stubs and napkins free
at any late-night cafe's kitchen door.

40 years I've put the words down
one
at
a
time

from wherever in my heart
they demanded release,
splayed in blood on paper
unrecognizable to child abusers.

F O U R

Aren't a good mother's arms
strong
when her child is in danger?

S E P T E M B E R 1 9 9 8 , N Y

MEET MOTHER

for all abused children,
teens, and adult victims
of child abuse

> *"Don't be ashamed of love.*
> *Show it.*
> *Always show it."*
>
> WILLIAM HOLDEN
> *film "The Earthling"*

ONE

First runner-up Miss America Pageant.
Pregnant with me.
Disqualified.
Blamed me.

An hour after birth
grasped my ankles,
turned

me

u
p
s
i
d
e

d
o
w
n

held my head

u
n
d
e
r

water of full bedside wash basin,
trying to drown me.

Unfortunately for me,

a passing nurse
calmly took me from mother
saying,
"I'll show you how to wash him,"
letting
it
go
at
that.

T W O

Never talked to me the 16 years
the court forced me to live with her.

T H R E E

Divorced trigger-tempered,
Marine sergeant father when 4,
introduced me to prison guard stepfather same
day.
Yanked all my teeth out with pliers
within an hour
as mother watched, sadistically smiling,
often repeating,
"he's not hurting you."

FOUR

How can a small child
possibly threaten adults?

FIVE

Throughout school years,
told teachers, principals, coaches,
anyone in authority
who could do something to stop the
unbelievable abuse,
or have me put in a foster home.

No one listened.
No one cared.
No one did anything
No one learned.

Never
crumbs
of
sabbath
bread.

Who
am
I
to
feel
I
deserve
love?

SIX

During the night
I left to tryout for the Cardinals,
walked softly to mother's bed,
kissed her cheek.
It was the first time
I had ever touched her.
I never saw her again.

SEVEN

Ten years ago I was told
stepfather drunkenly shoved her
down the basement stairs,
killing her,
and he's a prison lifer

who screams at night,
"I PUNISHED YOU FOR YOUR
OWN GOOD, JIMMIE!"

EIGHT

Jesus, did your religion fail?

PICNIC

Generous rounded hilltop
shaded by horse chestnut, sweet walnut,
white birch. Blanket spread over
wild chess down,
made cheerful by waving, sun-drenched,
long-necked yellow buttons.

Pleasing scent floats up:
prairie crab apple blossoms in
sheets of pink and white near a broad,
deep, two-track, once the passageway for
pioneer's steel-wheeled conestoga wagons;
oxen's heavy tread replaced by overgrown
weeds, thickets.

Do you see this?
Do you smell it?
Do you hear the creek back in the
bottom trees,
or the concerto of birds and frogs?
Are you deaf to your heartbeat,
and me walking up behind you?

4A Baseball IV

Playing field gone to tangles of
brush, briars, trees,
fighting for sun and root room.
Not a mark indicating
a ballpark was here.

Early '30s through late '50s,
baseball was better than life.
It was fair;
played in hundreds of small towns.

For the fan, there was a real sense of
being somebody when *his* team won,
lifting his heart—making him stronger
than his problems.

Opening day was special.
Every fan's team was in first place!
After a long winter
there was nothing like the smell and

first bite into a steaming dog or a
mouthful of hot popcorn!
Even the roving vendor's loud,
irritating voice was tolerable.
When the ump bellowed "PLAY BALL!"
shook the laziest of gods awake!

TWO

Players with Flaming Hearts
gone,
their names forgotten:

Snuffy Stirnweiss   Tommy O'Brien   Al Benton
Wayne Ambler   Rip Repulski   Gale Limmer
Nick Tremark   Cliff Chambers   John Sullivan
Lucky Lohrke   Don Plarski   Gene Crumling
Buster Mills   John Bolling   Nippy Jones
Tom Nelson   Al Wright   Debs Garms
Gordon Goldsberry   Bill Reed   Hugh Luby
Jim Fanning   Billy Bowers   Link Blakely

THREE

What killed the game?
In the 60s,

the complacent multi-millionaire
player's "club" was born.
Boyhood dreams of integrity in baseball,
guts to give *every* pitch your *whole* heart,
were traded in for six-figure salaries,
endorsements, investments.

Controlled by absurd amounts of money,
destroyed the ballpark that stood
triumphantly here,
and the hundreds like it.
Can't hear the trees creak and rub,
fighting for their position;
can't hear the chatter of wild birds,
witness
a
goshawk riding
soft,
reddish-pink
and
lavender
sunset updrafts,
as ball fans begin arriving
to watch the game their whole day
has been lived for...

If You Ask For A Lot,
Expect It To Cost A Lot

for Flip Ahrens

ONE

Naive unpublished female poet
dressed right out of '66,
talking to Gotham Book Mart's buyer,
wants to know what Manhattan publishers
to send her poetry manus to
from the Iowa village she lives in.

Said he didn't know,
suggesting she move here,
meet with agents, editors.

TWO

At an unexpected moment,
when opening a boxed gift:
thick, fluffy, white bath towels,
reminds her of the New York hotel

she stayed in—and the gamble not taken,
tells herself it was New York's loss,
not hers.

Whether she sees it or not,
each afternoon, the cutting board's
edge
wears down to just
"one   more   day."

To Inactive Christians

Believe you are Christian
simply because you actively
do no harm?
Think prayers are performance?
Worship, commitment?
Tithes, cross to salvation?
Isn't what the heart and emotions
do
makes the substance of the
real person?

Religion is easy.
Sacrificing safe, ordinary personal
and professional advantages, benefits,
agreeing with the crowd, and feelings
of well-being, are bare-bone tests.

Christ never said, *Adore me.*
He did say,
Pick up your cross and follow me.
What is he asking?

Risking questions,
acting upon them,
will lift you to a higher place,
summoning gifts didn't know you had,
deepening, strengthening you.

In a country peopled with
pious bigots, double-standards, masks,
why did I bother to write this poem?

*Oh where is the sharp-tailed grouse
and horned lark, to carry me from this
foolishness?
When a child, I wanted always to believe
the sun is carried across the sky
on the back of a turtle,
and the moon really is made of cheese.*

*Now I am a sensitive man.
I know emotional maturity means
giving from my heart,
not getting.*

*All falseness gone!
Skin breathes clean!
There were no bargain basement sales*

coming this far.
To turn away would be to destroy who I am.
How can anyone discover
themself
breathing what others have
exhaled?

Miniature Rain People

formed against
lonely
bedroom windows
windshields

When they cry
they
cry
them-
selves
all
away

Alone
in
the
night
everything
is
as
relevant
or

as
distant
as
you
want
it

The Poet Tries To Make Peace
With A Ruthless Tragedy
He Wasn't Responsible For

One is punished most
for one's virtues

NIETZSCHE

ONE

Beginning to step from
stopped, empty passenger train car,
Grand Central Terminal,
March 17, 1992,
to keep appointment with
screenwriting agent,
speeding, recklessly driven
baggage carrying truck
inside wide yellow line,
inches from train,
SMASHES

into poet's entire left side,
hurling him against train!
BOUNCES!
SLAMMED into second time!
Lifted higher!
Thrown, so when falling,
struck again!
CRASHES to cement in front of truck!
Truck brakes next to pleading,
critically injured poet.
Driver won't budge from seat.
Spits into victim's face!
Curses him!
Blames him!

T W O

FOOL!
HOW COULD YOU POSSIBLY SEE
GOLD
IN
THE
SUN,
SIMPLE
SILVER
IN

THE
STARS!
ALWAYS KNOWING WHEN
SNAKES SING AT NIGHT!

THREE

What is it you see then?
Is it a bad dream, a hallucination?
Is it a vision?
What is it you hear?

MARGARET ATWOOD

Permanently crippling the poet's sciatica,
left leg,
next four years became drug addict
taking prescribed medications to
partially relieve unbearable, constant
pain.

Living so deeply in heart,
feelings always true.
Spoken, written words of letters,
asking for simple humane kindness,
refused or ignored.

The few loved, physically healthy people
he trusted,
expected him to talk and act as they did.

No one wept with him.

No one encouraged him.

Rejecting him,
each denied he existed.

Worse.
Not witnessing his suffering,
sharing it,
none would ever know
what that sharing could have taught them.

Was it during periods of delirium,
or,
from somewhere else,
he knew Heaven was just the other side
of a short, lush green uprising
he was climbing,
the traditional Christian Christ
standing in his path, arm outstretched,
palm open, fingers together, pointing up,

caused the poet to smile, ask,
Are you a traffic cop?
Christ did not reply.
This silence prevented his entrance.

Twice, Saint Paul kissed him.
He saw a distant profile of
God's face,
seemingly in another universe.

F O U R

Sensing his mind was being altered
by the medications,
knowing he did his best writing when sober,
he didn't want it to happen where
the
word
was
impossible
to
write.
Quit drugs cold turkey, September 12, 1996.

Without initiated, guided, voiced
simple tenderness, understanding and support,
must
his
suffering,
and
feeling
he
doesn't
matter,
remain
invisible
except to crows
standing lordly over fresh meat
they did not kill?

12-97 through 7-98

He Knew Something Only A Few Others Do

for Jerry Williams
1938-1998

O N E

There was no disparity
between his inner and outer self.
A true response with his authentic
deeper self, gave him the freedom
to believe we are all one.

In no way a do-gooder or ass-kisser,
he was genuinely sensitive, fair,
big-hearted, enthusiastic, loyal,
honorable,
which caused guarded, repressed,
dishonest people,
to lie and ridicule him.

He protested unenforced
child abuse laws,

injustices to the poor,
damage and destruction committed
against the earth, the air, the
ozone layer.

T W O

Beginning at 12,
without intending to be there,
he was often where human life
was threatened. By 60,
he had saved more babies, children,
teens and adults in public swimming
pools, lakes, building fires,
vehicle collisions, and suicide attempts,
than men drink alcohol during a
hard drinking bout.
Many died in his arms, and before he
could get to them.
Once.
Just
once,
he was thanked:
a coast-to-coast trucker,
Pocono Mountains, I-80 West.

In his suffering caused by rejection,
he learned character is developed
not by intelligence, but by an
independent quality.

THREE

Jerry Williams died saving
a tenement family.
A beam fell, pinning him.
He suffocated.
No one claimed his body.
Why should they?
He wasn't like everyone else.
This is uninvolved, immature
adolescent America,
a country of self-serving neurotics,
who worship the superficial.

FOUR

What is it going to take
before it's learned
and acted upon,
the trouble isn't in the
emotionally healthy individualists

we make our enemies,
but within ourselves?

I'm Going To Be There With This
Poem When She Shines On Clear
Glass Like All Special Individuals
We Should Let Make A Difference

ONE

College dances,
virgin bright as Maypole streamers,
becomes blurred flames in bursts electric
beyond rhythms heavily accented
amplified beats,
sends my cock panting.

Ballads effortless,
liquid.
Angel of tenderness
softening my constant unbearable pain,
suffering.

T W O

Older, to keep going, to keep
our hearts alive,
don't we learn to believe in a lot
we
can't
touch?

Often a simple teaspoon of sugar,
my only sense of beauty...

SHOOT FOR THE STARS, DON'T SETTLE FOR THE CEILING

There's
always
a
limit.
We don't know what it is,
or
when
it
will
come.

Each time it happens
doesn't
not trying
for
what
we
think
can't be done,
kill

what
we
could
have
become?

Strong character, integrity,
doomed.
Cheap, inescapable denial
the ally to survival,
leaving
no
room
for
miracles
to
unfold.

Not even God can give back
what was given up.

J AM E S   H UM P H R E Y was born in a taxi during a blizzard

February 20, 1939, Sioux City, Iowa. Fiercely abused

physically night and day, as well as neglected when a baby

until his mid-teens, by his beautiful mother (Miss Iowa),

trigger-tempered Marine Corps sergeant father, and prison

guard stepfather, Jim began breaking the vicious abuse

cycle when 5, by telling any adult who would listen to

what was being done to him. No one aided him. For the

last 10 years, he has counseled abused homeless children,

orphans, runaways, and adult victims of child abuse in

Manhattan ghettos. He is a Brown University honors

graduate, M.A., Creative Writing, 1977.

His wife of 32 years, Norma Van Vooren-Humphrey,

to whose father, Charles Van Vooren (1902-1956), Humphrey dedicated *Bud* (Poets Alive! Press, 1996) is a New York reference librarian. There is one poem dedicated to the memory of Mr. Van Vooren in this book. Jim and Norma's only child, Saroyan, named after William Saroyan, lives in Seattle, where he is a freelance art director and designer.